Animals in Their Habitats

Mountain Animals

Francine Galko

Heinemann Library
Chicago, Illinois

Designed by Ginkgo Creative
Printed in China by South China Printing Company

07
10 9 8 7 6 5

Library of Congress Cataloging-in-Publication Data
Galko, Francine.
  Mountain animals / Francine Galko.
    p. cm. -- (Animals in their habitats)
Includes bibliographical references (p.   ).
Summary: Explores the animals who make their habitat in the mountains.
  ISBN 1-4034-0180-2 (HC), 1-4034-0437-2 (Pbk.)
  ISBN 978-1-4034-0180-9 (HC), 978-1-4034-0437-4 (Pbk.)
  1. Mountain animals--Juvenile literature. 2. Mountains--Juvenile
literature. [1. Mountain animals.] I. Title.
  QL113 .G25 2002
  591.75'3--dc21
                                    2001007656

Acknowledgments
The author and publishers are grateful to the following for permission to reproduce copyright material:
Cover photograph by George D. Lepp/Photo Researchers, Inc.
p. 4 Keith Gunnar/Bruce Coleman Inc.; p. 5 David Weintraub/Photo Researchers, Inc.; p. 6 R. Price/OSF/Animals Animals; p. 7 Francois Gohier/Photo Researchers, Inc.; p. 8 Darren Bennett/Animals Animals; p. 9 Michael Habicht; p. 10 Ken M. Johns/Photo Researchers, Inc.; p. 11 John Elk III/Bruce Coleman Inc.; p. 12 Dwight Kuhn; p. 13 Jim Zipp/Photo Researchers, Inc.; p. 14 C. K. Lorenz/Photo Researchers, Inc.; p. 15 Patti Murray/Animals Animals; p. 16 James H. Robinson/Animals Animals; p. 17 Johnny Johnson/Animals Animals; p. 18 Leonard Lee Rue III/Animals Animals; p. 19 Shane Moore/Animals Animals; p. 20 Art Wolfe; p. 21 George D. Lepp/Photo Researchers, Inc.; p. 22 Erwin and Peggy Bauer/Animals Animals; p. 23 Joe McDonald/Bruce Coleman Inc.; p. 24T Steve Valley; p. 24B Dennis Paulson; p. 25 Joe McDonald/Animals Animals; p. 26 David Boyle/Animals Animals; p. 27 Frans Lanting/Minden Pictures; p. 28 R. N. Mariscal/Bruce Coleman Inc.; p. 29 Bob and Clara Calhoun/Bruce Coleman Inc.
Every effort has been made to contact copyright holders of any material reproduced in this book. Any omissions will be rectified in subsequent printings if notice is given to the publisher.

Some words are shown in bold, **like this.** You can find out what they mean by looking in the glossary.

To learn more about the pika on the cover, turn to page 21.

Contents

 # What Are Mountains?

A mountain is a kind of **habitat**. Mountains are the highest places on Earth. Mountains can be as high as 600 school buses stacked end-to-end. Some mountains have **valleys** between them.

The sides of a mountain are often steep. The top of a mountain is called the **peak.** Some mountain peaks have snow on them all year.

Mountains are all over the world. Some mountains form where **volcanoes** have **erupted.** At first, a volcano forms a pile of hot rock. Over time, the rocks become a mountain.

Other mountains come from under the
ground. Deep inside Earth, the ground
moves very slowly. It pushes up mountains.
This takes a very long time, so you cannot
feel it or see it happen.

 # Mountain Homes

Many animals live on mountain **slopes.**
In spring, elk move up mountains to
meadows. In fall, they move down to the
foothills. They eat grasses and twigs.

Slate-colored fox sparrows nest in the trees
on the sides of mountains. They look for food
on the ground. They eat spiders and **insects.**

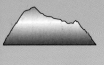 # Living Near the Bottom of a Mountain

As you go up a mountain, the land and the plants change. But at the bottom, the land does not change. Here, pronghorns **graze** on grasses and bushes.

Bison also live here. They graze on grasses near the bottoms of mountains. In the summer, they sometimes go up mountains to grassy **meadows**.

A water shrew dives to the bottoms of mountain streams. When it dives, air bubbles get caught in its fur. If it stops swimming, the air bubbles force the water shrew back to the **surface**.

American dippers live along mountain
streams. They dive into streams and walk
along the bottoms to catch **insects.** They
build their nests close to the water.

# Living in Mountain Trees

Trees grow on the lower part of mountain **slopes.** Here, Abert squirrels build nests high up in pine trees. Their strong claws and back legs help them climb up the tallest trees.

Clark's nutcracker birds nest in the trees on the sides of tall mountains. They eat the seeds in pine cones.

Living Above the Tree Line

Near the tops of mountains it is cold and there is little rain. Trees cannot grow above this **tree line.** Mountain goats live here. They have wool fur that keeps them warm.

Hoary marmots also live here. They whistle
loudly when they see a **predator,** such
as a coyote. This tells other marmots that
the predator is nearby.

Living in the Snow

Some mountains have snow on them.
Snowshoe hares live here. Their fur
turns white in winter. It helps them hide
in the snow. In the summer, their fur is
dark brown.

Grizzly bears live high up on mountains.
They **hibernate** in caves or underground.
They often dig **dens** in the sides of
mountains when there is deep snow.

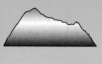 Finding Food on a Mountain

California condors live high up in the mountains. They fly around looking for large, dead animals. Condors do not hunt live animals.

Pikas eat grass that grows on the
mountainside. Sometimes they hide
grass under large rocks. When they
are hungry, they eat the hidden grass.

Mountain Predators

Some mountain animals are **predators.**
They hunt other animals on the mountains.
Mountain lions hunt mostly deer and rabbits.

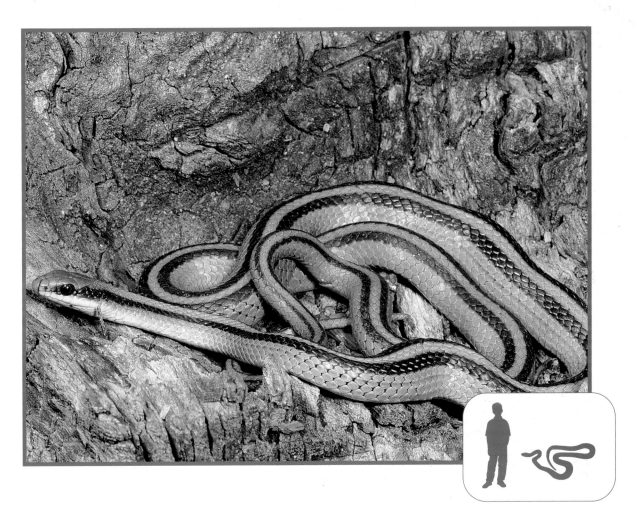

Mountain patchnose snakes live near the bottom of mountains. They eat lizards, rats, and other snakes. Sometimes they even eat snake eggs.

 # Hiding on a Mountain

Can you find the black petaltail in this picture? These **insects** are dragonflies. Their dark color helps them hide on tree trunks and leaves.

Seal salamanders live in cool, wet places on mountains. They usually hide under rocks during the daytime.

# Mountain Babies

Baby mule deer are born in mountain **meadows** in late spring or early summer. At first, they have white spots that help them hide from **predators.**

Baby peregrine falcons **hatch** in nests on high mountain cliffs. They can fly after just a month. As adults, peregrine falcons fly very fast.

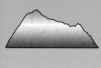 Protecting Mountain Animals

People have cut down the trees on mountains. Others have made roads through mountains. These things can cause mountain animals to lose their homes.

When you go to a mountain, stay on the trails. Do not leave **litter** or fires behind. Leaving mountains the way you found them helps protect the animals that live there.

 # Glossary

den animal's underground home

erupt to release hot air and rocks; to explode

foothill hill at the bottom of a mountain

graze to eat plants, such as grasses

habitat place where an animal lives

hatch to come out of an egg

hibernate to spend the winter resting

insect small animal with six legs

litter small pieces of trash

meadow grassy land

peak top part of a mountain

predator animal that hunts and eats other animals

slope side of a mountain

surface top of a stream or other body of water

tree line highest part of a mountain where trees can grow; trees cannot grow above this line

valley low area of land between mountains

volcano hole in the ground that hot rocks and air come out of

 # More Books to Read

Ashwell, Miranda and Andy Owen. *Mountains.* Chicago: Heinemann Library, 1998.

Dwyer, Jacqueline. *Mountains.* New York: PowerKids Press, 2000.

Fowler, Allan. *Cougar: Lion of the Mountains.* Danbury, Conn.: Children's Press, 1999.

Index